THE CANDIDATE

Word Processing Simulation

Second Edition

Ann Peele Ambrose, Dean
Business, Public Services, and Technologies
Tidewater Community College
Portsmouth, VA

THOMSON

SOUTH-WESTERN

Australia · Canada · Mexico · Singapore · Spain · United Kingdom · United States

THOMSON

SOUTH-WESTERN

The Candidate: Word Processing Simulation, 2E

Ann Peele Ambrose

VP/Editorial Director:
Jack W. Calhoun

VP/Editor-in-Chief:
Dave Shaut

Senior Publisher:
Karen Schmohe

Acquisitions Editor:
Jane Phelan

**Director Educational
Marketing:**
Carol Volz

Senior Marketing Manager:
Nancy Long

Marketing Manager:
Michael Cloran

Consulting Editor:
Diane Durkee

Editor:
Kim Kusnerak

Production Manager:
Tricia Boies

Sr. Print Buyer:
Charlene Taylor

Production House:
Cover to Cover
Publishing, Inc.

Printer:
Edwards Brothers
Ann Arbor, Michigan

Sr. Design Project Manager:
Michelle Kunkler

Cover/Internal Design:
Kim Torbeck/Imbue Design
Cincinnati, Ohio

Cover Photos:
Courtesy of
© Getty Images, Inc.

Permissions Editor:
Linda Ellis

The name of all products mentioned herein are used for identification purposes only and may be
trademarks or registered trademarks of their respective owners. South-Western disclaims any affil-
iation, association, connection with, sponsorship, or endorsement by such owners.

Microsoft® and Windows® are registered trademarks of Microsoft Corporation in the United States
and/or other countries.

Expect More from South-Western...
...and Get It!

SBI: Small Business Institute, Advanced Word Processing Simulation 2E This simple-to-use, advanced simulation is designed to reinforce word processing skills using documents such as letters, memos, reports, tables, programs, and newsletters. Composition, critical-thinking, and decision-making skills are also developed. This revision contains extended levels of applications that include most of the commonly used Word expert competencies and new tips that provide shortcuts and efficiencies of current Word software.

Simulation (softcover, 2-color, 128 pages)   0-538-43754-5

The Sports Connection 2E Reinforce essential applications skills for Office XP. This advanced simulation is different from other typical document-production simulations in that it provides students unique opportunities to go beyond the basics as they apply creativity in problem solving, decision making, flexibility, and more.

Simulation (softcover with CD, 2-color, 144 pages)   0-538-72765-9

Integrated Business Projects 2E This comprehensive computer projects text can be used in many situations. This project-based text applies word processing, spreadsheets, databases, presentations, and multimedia in 19 projects that range in difficulty from simple to complex. The text is set in Star River Adventures, a white-water rafting business. *Integrated Business Projects* can be used in a number of technology classes, from advanced keyboarding to computer applications.

Text (hardcover, side spiral, 4-color, 384 pages)   0-538-72762-4

Line Rollering 5E As employees at Westdale Line Rollering Club, students reinforce their beginning keyboarding and word processing skills by completing correspondence and other documents in this technology-based simulation. The Instructor CD contains data files for use with Microsoft® Word. (15+ hours)

Simulation (softcover, 2-color, 124 pages)   0-538-43425-2

CyberStopMedia.com: An Integrated Computer Simulation Students work through word processing, voice technology, spreadsheet, database, desktop publishing, and telecommunications activities in this completely integrated simulation. A CD with data files is included with each text. (30+ hours)

Text/Windows CD Package (hardcover, top spiral, 2-color, 96 pages)   0-538-72439-0

Century 21 Computer Applications & Keyboarding 7E Your tool for building a strong foundation based on time-tested keyboarding principles, while moving to the next level of comfort in the electronic world. The 7th Edition is designed to provide you with flexibility and choices:

- Complete coverage of computer applications: word processing, database, spreadsheet, speech recognition, electronic presentations, Web search, and Web design
- New-key learning lessons or keystroke review lessons – you choose where you want to begin
- Internet activities keep the content current and interactive
- Special features provide additional coverage of Skill Building, Word Processing, and Communication
- Applications build links to math, science, literature, and social studies
- Format guides and model documents throughout

Text (hardcover, top bound, 4-color, 608 pages)   0-538-69152-2

Join us on the Internet at www.swlearning.com

THOMSON

SOUTH-WESTERN

Contents

Introduction

ABOUT THE SIMULATION

The Candidate is a beginning word processing simulation designed to provide you with the opportunity to use your word processing skills in a realistic environment.

In this simulation your objectives are to:

★ format and process business documents such as letters, memos, reports, tables, news releases, flyers, minutes, and labels.

★ use basic word processing commands such as apply character styles, modify paragraph formats, create headers and footers, insert images and graphics, create documents from templates, manage files and folders, preview and print, use find and replace, and center page.

★ retrieve and edit stored files.

★ work from a variety of input including handwritten and rough draft.

★ conduct research on the Internet.

★ compose documents, think critically, and make decisions.

Job instructions are in the form of e-mails and handwritten notes. Some documents are already keyed and you will simply edit them. To assist you even further, a Reference Manual contains information such as a list of the data files, a summary of software commands, and sample documents, as well as a correlation of the simulation to the Microsoft® Word competencies.

WELCOME ABOARD!

We are happy to have you on the Elect Wright Campaign team! The campaign headquarters are located at 985 Cherryhill Crescent, Chesapeake, Virginia. Candidate William Wright, Jr., is following in his father's footsteps. His dad previously campaigned for and won both a city council seat and a state senate seat. Many of us worked on his father's campaign, and we are looking forward to getting young Candidate Wright elected as Mayor of Chesapeake.

Candidate Wright has many issues that he will focus on during his campaign. He believes, however, that regardless of the issues, if people don't come out to vote, nothing in the city will change. Thus, he has chosen the slogan, *What a difference "A" vote makes!* He plans to wage a fierce "get-out-to-vote" effort to encourage and empower everyone to vote, even if it is not for him. Every constituency in the city will feel the effects of his efforts.

One of the most important segments of the population that he will focus on is the young people of the city. He has decided that students need to be given an opportunity to share their concerns with him. Candidate Wright plans to invite them to get involved with his campaign in various ways. He has planned a summit meeting with students to enlighten them on the political process. He has also planned to hold a town meeting for students as well as visit their schools.

Candidate Wright is very pleased that you were selected to work on his campaign as an assistant to Markita Lawton, the campaign manager. You will shadow him (accompany him) to many functions and activities. This will give you first-hand experience with the political scene, which is very exciting. Candidate Wright is especially impressed with the essay you wrote that won you this opportunity; you expressed a keen insight into the political climate of our city.

In this unique experience, your responsibilities will be two-fold. You will have an opportunity to develop your word processing, composition, critical-thinking, and decision-making skills. Your responsibilities will include the office activities of running a campaign, such as handling correspondence, setting appointments, and scheduling appearances; preparing and reporting financial information; preparing news releases, schedules, tables, expense reports, and flyers; and other activities assigned to you by members of the Executive Campaign staff. You will also assist in preparing materials for the Summit. In addition, you will accompany the candidate to rallies, lunches, debates, and other meetings, and prepare reports, summaries, and other information requested by the candidate. Just think of all the people you will meet!

GENERAL DIRECTIONS

Read the guidelines below before you begin. Set up your folders as directed and then begin Job 1.

Reference Manual

Review the Reference Manual located in the back of this book before beginning. Most businesses adopt a standardized format to promote a corporate identity and to improve productivity. *The Candidate* follows this commonly accepted business practice.

Correspondence

A company letterhead template is provided on the data CD-ROM for use in preparing letters and memos. Save this letterhead as a document file using the job number. Review the standard formats for correspondence. Insert the current date on all documents for which a date is appropriate. Use the block letter format. Prepare an envelope for each letter unless your instructor gives you other directions.

A company logo has also been provided; use it to "dress-up" documents such as newsletters or news releases. A memo template has been provided for interoffice memos.

Time-Saving Tips

Use automated features to move within documents, to search and replace text, to verify and clear formatting, and to copy styles or formatting.

Insert page numbers on multipage documents. Insert a second-page heading on two-page letters or memos.

Data CD

To complete your assignments, you will use the data CD-ROM in the back of this text or obtain those files from your instructor. To install the files from the data CD, insert the CD into the drive. From the Start menu, select Run setup.exe. Follow prompts on the screen to complete the installation process. The files will automatically install by default to x:\Candidate (where *x* is your default drive letter). Simply open the files when you are ready to use them.

File Management

Store your solutions to the jobs in a well-defined file management system. You will be completing most of your work for the campaign manager, Markita Lawton, and a precinct chairperson, Victor McBride. Set up a folder for each of these persons; save all other documents in a third folder titled Other Projects. Should another individual have three or more documents for you to do, then create a new separate folder for this person, and move jobs to this folder.

Proofreading and Preparing Documents for Distribution

You are working as a professional, and as a professional, your documents must be error free. Establish a mindset that if a document contains errors, you will find them. Before submitting documents to your employer (instructor), follow these steps:

1. Read each job carefully before beginning to key it. Consult the Reference Manual and other available resources as necessary to obtain the information you need to complete the assignment. Remember:

   ★ The Reference Manual provides you with sample formats for various documents.

   ★ Tips provide additional instructions for completing the documents.

   ★ A CD icon alerts you to files stored on your data CD that you will need to retrieve in order to complete the jobs.

2. Create three folders and save them in whatever directory your instructor specifies. (For example, you may want to create the folders on drive A.) Remember, should another individual have three or more documents for you to do, then create a new separate folder for this person, and move jobs to this folder.

   Lawton
   McBride
   Other Projects

3. Save each job in the appropriate folder using the job number as the file name; for example, Job 01, Job 02, etc. Save each file in the appropriate folders as previously directed.

4. Proofread all documents to be sure they are error free.

   ★ Use the Spelling and Grammar checks.

   ★ Proofread on screen and correct errors not detected by the software; use the online thesaurus to enhance text.

   ★ Check placement and overall appearance in print preview.

   ★ Check the printed document with the source copy.

5. Print and assemble documents appropriately for final distribution.

6. After completing each job, record the date of completion in the Job Log in the Reference Manual section. When you receive your graded jobs from your instructor, record the grade in the appropriate space in the Job Log.

Campaign Information

ELECT WILLIAM WRIGHT, JR. CAMPAIGN

What A Difference "A" Vote Makes!

Headquarters: 985 Cherryhill Crescent

Chesapeake, Virginia 23322

Phone: (757) 555-0198

E-mail: wwright@electwrightjr.com

Campaign Staff:

Candidate	William Wright, Jr.
Campaign Manager	Markita Lawton
Student Volunteer	Student
Finance Chairperson	Michael Carruso
Treasurer	Jamie Romberg
Research Committee Chairperson	Carolyn Sheets
Public Relations Chairperson	Jason Tuber
Precinct/Volunteer Chairperson	Victor McBride
Event Planner	Loretta Nemtez
Scheduler	Carly Haymon

Jobs

From:	Markita Lawton [mlawton@electwrightjr.com]
To:	STUDENT [student@electwrightjr.com]
Date:	Wednesday, February 12, 200- 4:15 PM
Subject:	News Release for Youth Summit

We need to prepare a news release for the Youth Summit. Refer to the Reference Manual for the format.

Format the heading in Arial and right align as shown. Number the second page in the header position (upper right corner).

Thanks.

Elect William Wright, Jr. Campaign
985 Cherryhill Crescent
Chesapeake, Virginia 23322
(757) 555-0198
electwrightjr.com

TIP...

Refer to the Reference Manual for font sizes and styles.
Set a right tab to align the information in the heading.

SOFTWARE FUNCTIONS: Character Styles, Right Tab, Line Spacing, Page Numbers

News Release

Elect Wright Campaign
985 Cherryhill Crescent
Chesapeake, Virginia 23322
Contact Markita Lawton
Phone (757)555-0198

For immediate release

Chesapeake, VA, February 6, 200--- Candidate William Wright, Jr.
Hosts Youth & Politics Summit

The youth vote continues to decrease in each election! Why is this true? Is it because young people don't know how to vote? Is it because they don't understand the issues? Is it because they don't think that their vote will make a difference? Is it because politicians overlook this very important group of potential voters? Candidate Wright is not one of those politicians!

Candidate Wright understands the importance of the youth vote - today and in the future. He knows that our young people need to be involved with the issues of their communities because they will some-day be the leaders. He also understands that a concerted effort must be made to reach these young people, involved them in the process, and keep them involved. He also knows that it is just as important to address issues that are relevant to their votes.

Juniors and seniors in the city's high schools are invited to participate in a political summit designed especially for them. It—The summit will provide give them with an opportunity to share their opinions and concerns, discuss their issues, learn about the political process, interact with the candidate, register to vote, and even learn to use a voting machine!

The Youth & Politics Summit will be held on Saturday, (insert date two weeks from next Saturday), from 8:30 a.m. until 2:00 p.m. at the Greenbrier Conference Center. The admission is free. Contact your school counselor for registration and additional information.

From: Markita Lawton [mlawton@electwrightjr.com]
To: STUDENT [student@electwrightjr.com]
Date: Wednesday, February 12, 200- 7:12 PM
Subject: Flyer for Summit

I've drafted a flyer for the summit. Please see what you can do with it to make it attractive.   Format it using design elements such as color, lines, borders, etc. Insert clip art related to voting. Use an eye-catching font.

Thank you.

Elect William Wright, Jr. Campaign
985 Cherryhill Crescent
Chesapeake, Virginia 23322
(757) 555-0198
electwrightjr.com

TIP...

Size the graphic using the mouse.
Comic Sans MS is an example of a fancy, casual font.
Use 0.5" margins.

SOFTWARE FUNCTIONS: Character Effects, Clip Art, Page Border

Use a fancy font and a color

Youth & Politics Summit *(36 pt.)*

Use a second color here

Mayoral Candidate William Wright, Jr.
is hosting a
summit for high school juniors and seniors.

Use a check mark or a fancy bullet ↓

Insert a graphic related to voting here

The goals of the summit are to: *(18 pt.)*

- provide students with an opportunity to share and discuss their concerns and issues.
- help students understand the political process.
- give students the opportunity to register to vote and show them how to use a voting machine.
- encourage students to become involved in their community.

Vary the fonts; keep this on a single page

Saturday, *(date two weeks from Saturday)* *(18 pt.)*
8:30 a.m. until 2:00 p.m.
Greenbrier Conference Center
2020 Greenbrier Road
Chesapeake, Virginia

ADMISSION IS FREE

Contact high school counselors for additional information.

From: Markita Lawton [mlawton@electwrightjr.com]
To: STUDENT [student@electwrightjr.com]
Date: Thursday, February 13, 200- 8:12 PM
Subject: Summit Budget

I've left a handwritten copy of the Summit Budget file on your desk. Apply an attractive AutoFormat to the table.

Also include Decorations, $150; Donated.

Be sure to total expenses.

Thanks.

Elect William Wright, Jr. Campaign
985 Cherryhill Crescent
Chesapeake, Virginia 23322
(757) 555-0198
electwrightjr.com

TIP...

Use a formula to total expenses.
Format the total to include no zeros.

SOFTWARE FUNCTIONS: Table
AutoFormat, Tables
Formula, Number Format

YOUTH & POLITICS SUMMIT
Budget

Expense Item	Amount	Funding
Continental Breakfast for		
125 People	$1,200	Donated
Lunch for 125 People	1,825	Campaign Funds
Rental of Voting Machine	400	Donated
Decorations		
Prizes	300	Donated
Summit Materials	150	Campaign Funds
	Total	

From: Markita Lawton [mlawton@electwrightjr.com]
To: STUDENT [student@electwrightjr.com]
Date: Thursday, February 13, 200- 8:12 PM
Subject: Summit Program

Summit Program

I have drafted a program for the summit—set it up as attractively as you can. I'm also leaving a sample set up for you. The program will be printed front and back. Add clip art and a border to the first page.

Change the orientation to landscape and the margins to 0.5".

Format the program in two equal columns with a half-inch between columns.

Thanks.

Elect William Wright, Jr. Campaign
985 Cherryhill Crescent
Chesapeake, Virginia 23322
(757) 555-0198
electwrightjr.com

*Open Summit Program from the data files. Save it as Job 4.
Space information appropriately on pages. Preview the document and adjust the spacing so the program looks balanced.*

Summit Program

SOFTWARE FUNCTIONS: Columns, Modify Page Margins, Page Orientation, Borders, Clip Art

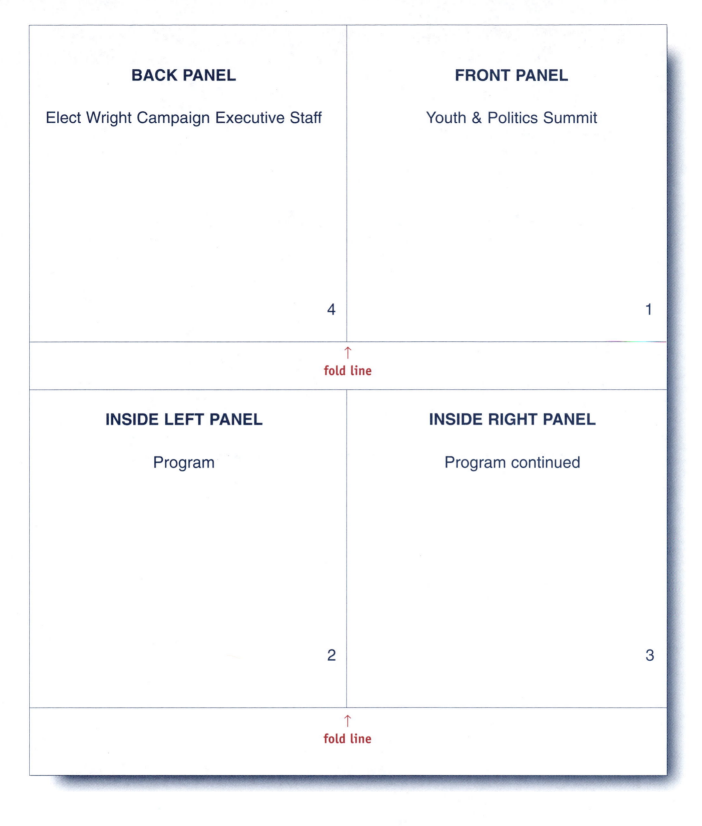

BACK PANEL

Elect Wright Campaign Executive Staff

4

FRONT PANEL

Youth & Politics Summit

1

↑
fold line

INSIDE LEFT PANEL

Program

2

INSIDE RIGHT PANEL

Program continued

3

↑
fold line

From: Betsy Ruiz [bruiz@electwrightjr.com]
To: STUDENT [student@electwrightjr.com]
Date: Friday, February 14, 200- 8:12 PM
Subject: Volunteer Thank-You Letter

I left a draft of the volunteer thank-you letter in the basket on your desk. Please key it on campaign letterhead (letterhead.dot). Check the Reference Manual for proper format.

Thank you.

Elect William Wright, Jr. Campaign
985 Cherryhill Crescent
Chesapeake, Virginia 23322
(757) 555-0198
electwrightjr.com

TIP...

Save Letterhead.dot as a document file (Job 5.doc).
Use the date command.
Insert a field for the address block (Insert, Field, Address Block).

Letterhead.dot

SOFTWARE FUNCTIONS: Date and Time, Field—Address Block

Insert Date

Insert a field for the address block

Dear Volunteer

Getting a candidate elected takes the work and cooperation of many people. Many details must be handled, many tasks must be completed, and many people need to be organized and managed. There is always a need for additional help.

Thank you for your spirit of volunteerism and your belief in our candidate, William Wright, Jr., for the mayor of our great city.

The next volunteer training session will be held on Saturday, February 22, at 10 a.m. at our headquarters building located at 283 Johnson Boulevard in the Olde Towne section of the city. During the training session, you will have an opportunity to discuss the activities in which you would like to be involved based on your talents and interests.

Again, thank you for volunteering to work with our campaign and we look forward to seeing you on Saturday, February 22, at 10 a.m.

Sincerely

Betsy Ruiz
Volunteer Chairperson

From: Markita Lawton [mlawton@electwrightjr.com]
To: STUDENT [student@electwrightjr.com]
Date: Monday, February 17, 200- 8:12 PM
Subject: Job Descriptions

          Job Descriptions

We need to update the job descriptions for the Procedures Manual. I have placed an edited copy of the current descriptions in your work basket.

Please retrieve the Job Descriptions file and make the changes indicated on the edited copy. Add leaders after each job title. Also on the second page, add the header *Job Descriptions* at the left and Page # at the right.

Thank you.

Elect William Wright, Jr. Campaign
985 Cherryhill Crescent
Chesapeake, Virginia 23322
(757) 555-0198
electwrightjr.com

Set a right leader tab at the right margin.

Job Descriptions

SOFTWARE FUNCTIONS: Right Leader Tab, Header/Footer

ELECT WRIGHT CAMPAIGN

Campaign Workers Job Descriptions

Right leader tab

CAMPAIGN MANAGER . . . . . .

The campaign manager's main responsibility is to make it possible for
the candidate *to* focus on his/her own responsibilities and not have to be
concerned about whether the campaign is being run properly but rather
focus on issues and maximize his/her time with the public. The campaign
manager assembles volunteers, schedules events, oversees public relations
efforts, and is responsible for anything and everything that is done in
the candidate's name. This person is also responsible for troubleshoot-
ing, setting priorities and assigning responsibility for individual jobs.

STUDENT ASSISTANT . . . . .

The student assistant is responsible for assisting the campaign manager
in all of his/her duties. In addition, the student assistant is responsible for maintaining the office, which includes preparing correspondence
and other types of documents as required by other members of the executive staff. The student assistant may also accompany the candidate to
various functions and meetings.

PERSON

FINANCE CHAIRMAN . . . .

This person must be able to understand money and have the ability to
raise it. He/She is responsible for fundraising. He/She should be re-
spected by potential contributors. The finance chairman *person* is responsible
for establishing a campaign budget and insuring that it is adhered to.
He/She
this person works very closely with the treasurer.

The treasurer
TREASURER   . . . .
This person is responsible for maintaining the bank accounts, including
writing checks for all expenditures.

Continued on page 14

RESEARCH COMMITTEE CHAIRPERSON . . . .

The research committee chairperson is responsible for researching past elections of the same type to ascertain information about issues and identify voters. This person is also responsible for obtaining information that could be used in the preparation of speeches. Analyzing the opponent's campaign is also a responsibility of the research committee chairperson.

PUBLIC RELATIONS
~~COMMUNICATIONS~~ CHAIRPERSON . . . . .

~~This~~ *The public relations* chairperson is responsible for preparing any communications needed by the campaign. These may include news releases, speeches, and campaign literature such as flyers and posters. ~~The chairperson is also responsible for scheduling activities.~~ *He/She maintains direct contact with the news media.*

SPECIAL GROUPS CHAIRPERSON . . . .

This person is responsible for identifying various groups that extra attention must be focused on in an effort to be sure that their issues are addressed.

PRECINCT/VOLUNTEER CHAIRPERSON. . . . .

The precinct/volunteer chairperson coordinates organizations and volunteers.

EVENT PLANNER . . . .

The event planner organizes rallies, dinners, coffees, banquets, and other events.

SCHEDULER . . . . . .

The scheduler maintains the calendar and daily event schedule. He/She initiates contacts with other friendly politicians who can provide information on events that the candidate may not be aware.

From: Markita Lawton [mlawton@electwrightjr.com]
To: STUDENT [student@electwrightjr.com]
Date: Wednesday, February 19, 200- 9:15 PM
Subject: Staff Meeting Minutes

I've left the minutes of the last staff meeting in your basket. I read over them and made corrections (make sure that I didn't miss any errors). Adjust the top margin to make this fit on one page.

Check the campaign information (page viii) for the members of the Executive Committee.

Thank you.

Elect William Wright, Jr. Campaign
985 Cherryhill Crescent
Chesapeake, Virginia 23322
(757) 555-0198
electwrightjr.com

TIP...

Use Word defaults to number the paragraphs.

Elect Wright Campaign
Staff Meeting Minutes
February 17, 200-, 10 a.m.

The weekly meeting of the campaign staff was held on February 17, 200-, at 10 a.m.

Attendance: All members of the Executive Committee (Include the names of all of the executive committee members except Jason Tuber, who was absent.)

Recorder of Minutes: Student Assistant

1. The campaign manager called the meeting to order at 10 a.m.

2. Written reports from the following committees, chairpersons, and officers were distributed, discussed, and approved or ~~excepted~~ accepted (copies were submitted to the recorder and campaign manager):

   A. Treasurer--Approved

   B. Finance Committee--Accepted

   C. Public Relations--Accepted

   D. Precinct/Volunteer Chair--Accepted

   E. Event Planner--Accepted

3. The following unfinished business was discussed and acted upon:

   A. Application for internship for Hampton Roads University student criteria was approved.

   B. Ticket price of $50 for awards dinner was approved.

4. The following new business was discussed/acted upon:

   A. New strategies were discussed. These will be summarized and distributed at next week's staff meeting.

Continued on page 17

B. Student town meeting was discussed. The idea was accepted by everyone. However, logistics need to be worked out. The public relations chair will work on this and report to the staff at next week's meeting.

5. The next meeting will be Monday, February 24, 200-. The meeting adjourned at 11:55 a.m.

From:	Markita Lawton [mlawton@electwrightjr.com]
To:	STUDENT [student@electwrightjr.com]
Date:	Wednesday, February 19, 200- 8:25 PM
Subject:	Campaign Issues

Campaign Issues

I am attaching a draft of Candidate Wright's campaign issues. Please prepare a final copy in report format.   Replace the word "citizen" with "people" each time it appears in the document.

Thank you.

Elect William Wright, Jr. Campaign
985 Cherryhill Crescent
Chesapeake, Virginia 23322
(757) 555-0198
electwrightjr.com

Change bullet style to a small square.

Campaign Issues

SOFTWARE FUNCTIONS: Bullets and Numbering, Find and Replace, Modify Tabs

2" top margin

CANDIDATE WRIGHT'S CAMPAIGN ISSUES *14 pt.*

Candidate Wright's roots are in Chesapeake, Virginia. He was born, raised, and educated in the city. He is what some may call "home grown." He has been involved in the life of the city all of his life. He has worked in various "governmental" capacities within his father's administration as well as in other administration *s and organizations.*

He is very concerned about the future of our city and feels that we need a new vision. He will ~~provide~~ *develop*, with the help of the citizens of Chesapeake, new solutions to problems that will make us "the model city." Candidate Wright believes that an accountable government system, a strong educational system, a healthy economy, a strong stand on crime, and strong and healthy families are the keys to a successful and strong community.

- Accountable Government *Use a square bullet; SS items; DS between*
    The citizens of the city have a right to know how their money is being spent. Any unnecessary and inappropriate spending must be identified and stopped ~~with~~ appropriate actions ~~being~~ taken.
    ^and *^must be*

- Education System   *All children,*
    will We support the national campaign, "No Child Left Behind." ~~Every child,~~ regardless of their level of learning, will be given the opportunity to learn so that they can become productive citizens. Partnerships with local businesses will be encouraged.

- Strong Economy
    Business is the lifeblood of any community. We must promote new industry based on a plan for economic development. As the economic base increases, we must support existing businesses that will encourage growth and small business ownership. We need to encourage new businesses that will provide job opportunities for local citizens.

Continued on page 20

- Crime

  Criminals must be punished! Those criminals who commit violent crimes should serve their full sentences without parole. In dealing with the crime problem, we need to educate our citizens and to identify activities that will focus on our youth, whose crime rate has increased over 25 percent in the last two years.

- Healthy Citizens

  All citizens of the city will have affordable health care. *to all citizens.* Health and welfare services will be provided. Enforcement of child support laws and teen pregnancy prevention programs will be supported. Laws protecting women, children, and families will be given priority with regard to funding and enforcement.

  Candidate Wright He feels that the only way that any change can take place in the city *is to* citizens must get involved and more importantly, vote. *its people* *get them to vote.* He wants the citizens to know that their individual vote will make a difference. A "get-out-the-vote" campaign will be forged to reach all citizens, *and* especially the young voters. His theme for this campaign is "What a difference "A" vote makes!"

  Candidate Wright has demonstrated his commitment to Chesapeake over the years through his involvement in many aspects of the life of the city. This commitment and his determination make him the best choice for "Mayor of Chesapeake!"

ELECT WILLIAM WRIGHT, JR. CAMPAIGN

FROM THE DESK OF MARKITA LAWTON

February 24

Candidate Wright wants to give a "quiz" at the upcoming town meeting for students. The winners will be treated to a limo ride to lunch at a selected fast food restaurant! I have attached a copy of the quiz that needs to be keyed in appropriate format.

Use WordArt for the title.

Thanks.

985 Cherryhill Crescent ★ Chesapeake, Virginia 23322 ★ (757) 555-0198 ★ E-mail:

TIP...

Number each question using a hanging indent. Double space between items. Make the write-on lines 1" long.

THE RIGHT VOTE *Use WordArt*

Just how politically savvy are you?

Set a right leader tab ↓

Name _____

School _____

DIRECTIONS: Write the correct answer in the space provided. *For the answer lines, set a right underline tab at 1"; then set a left tab at 1.25" and 1.5"*

_____ 1.   A person who is trying to get elected.

_____ 2.   A soldier stationed in a far away country on Election Day would use this to cast his/her vote.

_____ 3.   How old must you be to register to vote?

_____ 4.   Is it true that you can only vote for candidates whose names appear on the ballot?

_____ 5.   Can a felon vote?

_____ 6.   How old must you be to vote?

_____ 7.   A new president is elected in this month.

_____ 8.   The place where you go to vote.

_____ 9.   A group that shares the same views about government and works together to win elections.

_____ 10. A form you mark when you vote.

1"   1.25"   1.5"

Underline tab   Left tabs

"WHAT A DIFFERENCE "A" VOTE MAKES!"   *Bold and center*

From: Victor McBride [vmcbride@electwrightjr.com]
To: STUDENT [student@electwrightjr.com]
Date: Tuesday, February 25, 200- 9:15 AM
Subject: Civic League List

I've left a partial list of civic leagues on your desk. Please key the table in landscape format. Adjust the column widths so that all information for each league fits on one line (as shown). Add shading to the row containing the column headings. Use Arial font. Key heading lines within the table.

Thank you.

Elect William Wright, Jr. Campaign
985 Cherryhill Crescent
Chesapeake, Virginia 23322
(757) 555-0198
electwrightjr.com

TIP...

Create a 5-column, 9-row table. Bold and center align the heading row. Center the page.

Chesapeake Civic Leagues
Meeting Schedules

Civic League	President & Address	Telephone	Meeting Dates	Time
Greenhill	Ms. Rosalyn Sawyer 404 Dunston Street Chesapeake, VA 23325-4087	555-0132	2nd Monday	7 p.m.
Centerville	Ms. Mary Santos 6312 Sedgewater Drive Chesapeake, VA 23324-0488	555-0112	1st Tuesday	7 p.m.
West Landing	Mr. Robert Geddes 863 Gilmer Road Chesapeake, VA 23323-0372	555-0192	2nd Wednesday	7 p.m.
Western Branch	Mr. Dennis Ferrell 13 Wast Road Chesapeake, VA 23320-0328	555-0199	4th Thursday	7 p.m.
Newton	Ms. Cynthia Mendez 1024 Robindale Road Chesapeake, VA 23323-0431	555-0111	1st Monday	7 p.m.
Grassfield	Mrs. Sharon Tatum 1012 Castle Lane Chesapeake, VA 23325-0421	555-1834	2nd Monday	7 p.m.
Riverwalk	Mrs. Ruby Edwards 700 Pier Road Chesapeake, VA 23320-0422	555-0178	2nd Saturday	11 a.m.

February 26
Candidate Wright will be speaking at each of the high schools in the city during the week of March 10. Please key the attached schedule. Center it vertically on the page. Thanks.
ml

SPEAKING SCHEDULE FOR CITY'S HIGH SCHOOLS
Week of May 10-14, 200-

Date & Time	School & Address	Principal
Monday, March 10 1:30 p.m.	Chesapeake High School 238 Greenbrier Landing Chesapeake, VA 23323 (757) 555-0149	Mr. Jesse Smith
Tuesday, March 11 12:45 p.m.	Eastern Branch High School 1954 Roosevelt Crescent Chesapeake, VA 23324 (757) 555-0170	Mrs. Gwen Newton
Wednesday, March 12 10:45 a.m.	Indian Cove High School 173 Whittier Street Chesapeake, VA 23320 (757) 555-0124	Dr. Barbara Cooper
Thursday, March 13 11:15 a.m.	Grassfield High School 314 Blount Street Chesapeake, VA 23321 (757) 555-0118	Ms. Phyllis Chang
Friday, March 14 2:05 p.m	Oscar Green High School 2003 Newton Drive Chesapeake, VA 23325 (757) 555-0108	Dr. Paul Glaser

TIP...

Set a tab at 2.0" and 4.5" to align the information or set it up as a table.

From: Markita Lawton [mlawton@electwrightjr.com]
To: STUDENT [student@electwrightjr.com]
Date: Monday, March 3, 200- 1:12 PM
Subject: School Board Meeting Report

    School Board Meeting

I read your report on your visit to the School Board Meeting with Candidate Wright. See the comments I added with corrections/suggestions. Delete the comments when you finish. Please print two copies. Hope you enjoyed the meeting.

Thank you.

Elect William Wright, Jr. Campaign
985 Cherryhill Crescent
Chesapeake, Virginia 23322
(757) 555-0198
electwrightjr.com

Format this as a report. Refer to the Reference Manual if necessary.

School Board Meeting

SOFTWARE FUNCTION: **Comments**

From: Jason Tuber [jtuber@electwrightjr.com]
To: STUDENT [student@electwrightjr.com]
Date: Tuesday, March 4, 200- 10:39 AM
Subject: News Release Information

      News Release

I have attached a document containing information for a news release. Please format the news release correctly.

Thank you.

Elect William Wright, Jr. Campaign
985 Cherryhill Crescent
Chesapeake, Virginia 23322
(757) 555-0198
electwrightjr.com

*Use an em dash between
the date and the message.
(Insert, Symbol, Special
Characters, Em dash.)*

News Release

ELECT WILLIAM WRIGHT, JR. CAMPAIGN

FROM THE DESK OF LORETTA NEMTEZ

March 5

Please key the list of activities as a memo to Carly Haymon, Scheduler.

Leave copies on my desk.

Thanks.

Loretta

TIP...

Refer to the Reference Manual for the correct memo format.

985 Cherryhill Crescent ★ Chesapeake, Virginia 23322 ★ (757) 555-0198 ★ E-mail: electwrightjr.com

Memo.dot

Below is a description of two activities that we will be sponsoring soon at each of the city high schools. I am in the process of planning and scheduling them now. Please review the list and let me have any ideas, suggestions, or concerns.

Rallies

The student body will hold a pep rally during their regular activity hour. All of the candidates for mayor will be on hand to meet the "youth" voters. Each candidate will be introduced and given an opportunity to speak to the students. This will give candidates an opportunity to make their issues and concerns known to the students. A representative from the Electoral Board will be on hand to give information regarding registering to vote. Literature regarding voter registration will be available. An actual registration drive will be held later in the year at each high school. Additional activities at the rally include pep songs, cheering, prizes, balloons, etc.

Fundraisers

Each school is in the process of identifying a fundraiser within its school. It seems that each one is planning a contest among each of the senior homerooms. Each homeroom will participate in a different fundraiser. Our campaign will provide the prize. If you have any additional ideas for this activity, please let me know.

I look forward to your comments.

From: Victor McBride [vmcbride@electwrightjr.com]
To: STUDENT [student@electwrightjr.com]
Date: Monday, March 10, 200- 11:12 AM
Subject: Instructions for Precinct Leaders

    Precinct Leaders

Please retrieve the attached document and make the changes indicated on the copy I left on your desk.

Thanks.

Elect William Wright, Jr. Campaign
985 Cherryhill Crescent
Chesapeake, Virginia 23322
(757) 555-0198
electwrightjr.com

Precinct Leaders

SOFTWARE FUNCTION: Bullets and Numbering

1" top margin INSTRUCTIONS FOR PRECINCT LEADERS **14 pt.**

Our objective is to get William Wright, Jr., elected as mayor of Chesapeake. This means that our main function is to get as many voters as possible who favor William Wright, Jr., to come to the polls and ~~VOTE~~ *lc* on Election Day, ~~November 4~~ **May 7**. We believe it will take 45,000 votes for Wright to be elected. To achieve this goal, there are certain things we must do:

SS the numbered list and DS between; use 0.25" hanging indent

1. Canvass ALL of the REGISTERED VOTERS in each precinct (either by phone or in person). Suggested procedure is attached.

2. Secure poll workers for Election Day, ~~November 4th~~ **May 7**. Plan to have at least TWO people working the polls and giving out William Wright, Jr., materials at ALL TIMES during the day from 6 a.m. to 7 p.m. It is suggested that workers are assigned in two-hour shifts.

3. Schedule TELEPHONE CALLERS for ~~October 30 – November 4~~ **April 10 through May 7** to call those who favor William Wright, Jr. This call may be made by the person previously calling or by a different team of workers. This call is a REMINDER TO VOTE call.

4. Encourage all UNREGISTERED VOTERS to register to vote by the deadline.

5. Keep a record of voters who are UNDECIDED. Give this record to the volunteer coordinator each week on Wednesday beginning ~~October 15~~ **April 13**.

6. Participate in "coffees" and special events in your precinct. If needed, assist in planning such events.

7. Identify workers willing to participate in a "neighborhood blitz" on the last two Saturdays in ~~October~~ **April**.

↓ 3

Thank you all for your commitment and your efforts to elect William Wright, Jr., as Mayor of Chesapeake.

"What a Difference "A" Vote Makes!" **14 pt.; bold and center**

From: Markita Lawton [mlawton@electwrightjr.com]
To: STUDENT [student@electwrightjr.com]
Date: Thursday, March 13, 200- 2:15 PM
Subject: Outline

Please key the school violence outline that I left on your desk. I want to use it to prepare a presentation later that I will give.

Thanks.

Elect William Wright, Jr. Campaign
985 Cherryhill Crescent
Chesapeake, Virginia 23322
(757) 555-0198
electwrightjr.com

TIP...

Set a decimal tab at 0.25" to align the Roman numerals. Press tab before you key the first Roman numeral. Then set tabs every 0.25" to align the remaining text.

SOFTWARE FUNCTION: Decimal Tab

VIOLENCE IN OUR SCHOOLS *14 pt.*

I. FACTS ABOUT SCHOOL VIOLENCE

A. Over 25 percent of public schools reported at least one serious crime

B. Eighty-five young people died violently in U.S. schools

C. Seventy-five percent of these deaths involved guns

D. Location is not a factor in school violence

II. CAUSES OF VIOLENCE

A. Preoccupation with violence
  1. Playing violent video games, listening to violent music
  2. Collecting weapons

B. Family history
  1. Violence in the home
  2. Child abuse
  3. Excessive punishment
  4. Dysfunctional families

C. Social status and surroundings
  1. Availability of drugs and guns
  2. Economic deprivation
  3. Gangs
  4. Drugs and alcohol
  5. Entertainment industry

III. PREVENTION STRATEGIES

A. Family therapy

B. Conflict resolution training

C. Drug education

D. Violence prevention counseling

E. Bullying reduction

F. School security patrol

G. Peer mediation

From: Markita Lawton [mlawton@electwrightjr.com]
To: STUDENT [student@electwrightjr.com]
Date: Friday, March 14, 200- 10:24 AM
Subject: Budget

Summit Budget

Use the information in the Summit Budget data file to create a chart of expenses from the data in the first two columns. Then compose a memo to Jamie Romberg telling him that the budget for the Youth Summit is included along with a chart.

Thanks.

Elect William Wright, Jr. Campaign
985 Cherryhill Crescent
Chesapeake, Virginia 23322
(757) 555-0198
electwrightjr.com

TIP...

To create the chart, select Insert, Object, Create New, and Microsoft Graph Chart. Key a main word for each item in the legend.

Summit Budget

SOFTWARE FUNCTION: *Create Chart*

From: Markita Lawton [mlawton@electwrightjr.com]
To: STUDENT [student@electwrightjr.com]
Date: Thursday, March 13, 200- 2:15 PM
Subject: Job Descriptions

Open the Job Descriptions (Job 6) file and add the names of persons filling those positions. I've left the names on your desk. Leave the first two positions as they are; then reorder the remaining positions so that the position titles are in alphabetical order. Apply full justification to the body.

Change line spacing of the body to 1.5. Change the spacing above the second heading to 12 points. Then apply this format to the remaining job description headings.

Thanks.

Elect William Wright, Jr. Campaign
985 Cherryhill Crescent
Chesapeake, Virginia 23322
(757) 555-0198
electwrightjr.com

TIP...

Use Keep with Next to ensure that headings stay with the copy that follows.
Double-click the format and use Format Painter to apply the format to remaining headings.

SOFTWARE FUNCTIONS: Cut and Paste, Keep with Next, Spacing Before/After Paragraph, Format Painter

Campaign Manager, Markita Lawton

Student Assistant, Your Name

Event Planner, Loretta Nemtez

Finance Chairperson, Michael Carruso

Precinct/Volunteer Chairperson, Victor McBride

Public Relations Chairperson, Jason Tuber

Research Committee Chairperson, Carolyn Sheets

Scheduler, Carly Haymon

Treasurer, Jamie Romberg

From: Markita Lawton [mlawton@electwrightjr.com]
To: STUDENT [student@electwrightjr.com]
Date: Thursday, March 18, 200- 8:17 AM
Subject: Newsletter

      Newsletter

I have keyed the information for the newsletter. Please open the file and format the information in three columns. Use various design elements to add some excitement. Print one copy. Revise the newsletter to have two columns. Print one copy. Save this two-column version with a different file name.

Thanks.

Elect William Wright, Jr. Campaign
985 Cherryhill Crescent
Chesapeake, Virginia 23322
(757) 555-0198
electwrightjr.com

TIP...

Set left and right margins at 1". Use the column feature to arrange text in two columns. Add graphics, lines, WordArt, etc.

Newsletter

From: Victor McBride [vmcbride@electwrightjr.com]
To: STUDENT [student@electwrightjr.com]
Date: Tuesday, March 18, 200- 8:12 PM
Subject: Thank-you Letter for Contributions

Please key the attached letter to the superintendent and give it to me with an addressed envelope.

Thank you.

Elect William Wright, Jr. Campaign
985 Cherryhill Crescent
Chesapeake, Virginia 23322
(757) 555-0198
electwrightjr.com

TIP...

Use the letterhead template.
Add a second-page header.

SOFTWARE FUNCTIONS: Envelopes and Labels, Header

Date

Dr. Taylor M. Baldwin, Superintendent
Chesapeake Public Schools
School Board Building
787 Cedar Road
Chesapeake, VA 23323

Dear Dr. Baldwin

If you have been following my campaign, you know that I am very interested in the youth of our city and getting them involved in city politics. I know that our young people are also very important to you.

The youth of our city are the future leaders of Chesapeake. It is extremely important that we empower them so that they are ready to fill any government positions that will be vacated by those of us who have served for many years. In order to accomplish this goal, we must prepare our youth and provide them with the opportunities for understanding the roles and responsibilities of those who make policy decisions in the city government, in city development, and in the educational system. We cannot wait until our young people become "middle aged" to begin educating and training them so that they can assume many of these responsibilities.

Students need to have an opportunity for meaningful involvement in educational decisions, especially those that affect them and their schools. They need to become more aware of the many elements that enter into making certain decisions. They also need to understand the consequences of these decisions. We can accomplish this by creating two slots on the local school board for young people; one female and one male. They would be elected to the school board by their fellow students and they would represent the

Continued on page 40

diversity and power of youth in the city. They would attend all regular school board meetings and participate in all discussions, panels, etc., as conventional school board members. However, even though they will have the opportunity to share their opinions and concerns, they will not be permitted to vote on issues.

I would like to discuss this project in more detail with you. It would be wonderful if the entire school board could be involved with us in this discussion so that we gather their support. Please contact me at your earliest convenience so that we can schedule a meeting. I believe that our great city would benefit significantly from this endeavor. Students will feel that they are truly an important element of our great city and we will be training them for the future—a win-win situation for everyone.

Sincerely

William Wright, Jr.
Candidate

From: William Wright, Jr. [wwright@electwrightjr.com]
To: STUDENT [student@electwrightjr.com]
Date: Friday, March 21, 200- 10:40 AM
Subject: Report

Absentee Voting

Please retrieve the attached document and format it as a report. You will probably need to insert page breaks, change margins, spacing, etc. I also inserted some notes on the document. I've left the text for the title page on your desk. Prepare this as a separate document and make it attractive. Save the title page as Job 21T.

Thanks.

Elect William Wright, Jr. Campaign
985 Cherryhill Crescent
Chesapeake, Virginia 23322
(757) 555-0198
electwrightjr.com

TIP...

Be sure that headings stay with the paragraphs that follow. Use WordArt, graphics, special fonts, and color for the title page.

Absentee Voting

Absentee Voting   **WordArt**

Presented to

High School Assemblies

by

William W. Wright, Jr.

CANDIDATE FOR MAYOR OF CHESAPEAKE

June 5, 200-

From: Markita Lawton [mlawton@electwrightjr.com]
To: STUDENT [student@electwrightjr.com]
Date: Friday, March 21, 200- 10:48 PM
Subject: Certificate

Certificate

Use the information in the attached document to create an attractive certificate in landscape orientation. I've included a graphic of an official seal. Use it if you can. You may find another graphic if you wish or not use one at all. I've left a sample certificate on your desk.

Thanks.

Elect William Wright, Jr. Campaign
985 Cherryhill Crescent
Chesapeake, Virginia 23322
(757) 555-0198
electwrightjr.com

Set 0.5" margins. Use a fancy border around the certificate. Use WordArt and change the font styles and effects so the certificate is attractive.

Certificate

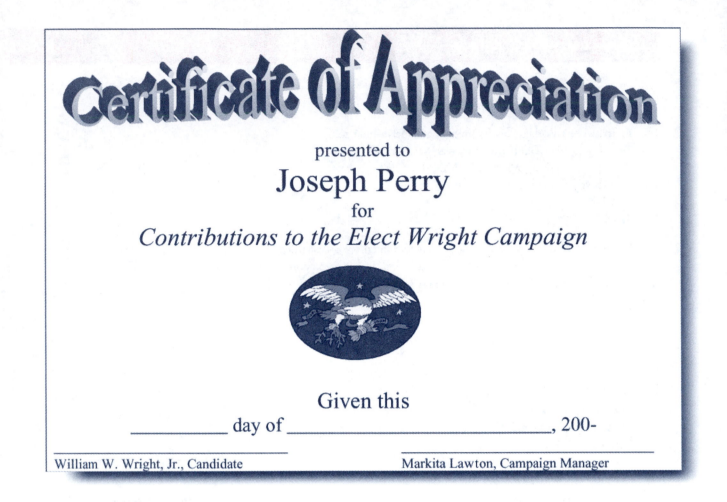

Certificate of Appreciation

presented to

Joseph Perry

for

Contributions to the Elect Wright Campaign

Given this

_____ day of _____, 200-

_____   _____
William W. Wright, Jr., Candidate   Markita Lawton, Campaign Manager

3/24
Need mailing labels for this list.
Use Avery 5160 labels. These
people are all from Chesapeake.
Include the city and state, and
the title Mr. or Ms. for each
name.
   Thanks.
   ml

Jessica Coles	Jose Valdez	Andrew Haywood
107 Miller Crescent	907 Deep Creek Boulevard	777 Signet Quay
Chesapeake, VA 23323	23322	23325
Clara James	Paul Schwartz	Diane Holton
203 Apple Tree Lane	7513 Thurston Road	120 College Place
23323	23321	23322
Tia Davis	Neil Cherry	Leonard Cage
104 Bayside Drive	213 Arthur Street	418 Central Drive
23320	23325	23324
Mark Turner	Peggy Yates	Shelley DeVault
274 Oakside Court	412 Portsmouth Boulevard	419 25th Street
23321	23320	23326

Continued on page 46

TIP...

Use Letters and Mailings feature. Don't forget to select New Document to key the labels.

SOFTWARE FUNCTION: *Labels*

George Haynes
1562 Butler Road
23320

Tayra Manuelito
304 Masters Lane
23323

Marie Shoemaker
333 Richmond Road
23323

Adam Yang
26 Grove Crescent
23321

Jeremiah Perkinson
212 Alston Street
23325

Richard Powell
700 Shirlington Place
23324

Dalton Riveria
354 Piney Ridge Way
23324

Charles Mills
416 Corporate Crossing
23320

Morris Kennedy
872 Center Road
23320

Lois Carmichael
678 Stoney Island Lane
23322

Michael Lamb
467 Terry Lane
23321

Paul Sigman
760 Beach Lane
23326

Craig Massey
136 Templeton Quay
23320

Rusty Shannon
900 Garden Lane
23320

Charlene Davis
110 Calvary Crescent
23321

Mrs. Tess Spence
208 Pugh Road
23321

Andrew Reese
808 Dunbarton Road
23326

Jackson DiMario
Two Seaside Place
23321

From: Victor McBride [vmcbride@electwrightjr.com]
To: STUDENT [student@electwrightjr.com]
Date: Thursday, March 27, 200- 11:20 PM
Subject: Instructions for Telephone Callers

📎   Telephone Script

The students at the high school have organized a telephone poll. They are calling students to determine their issues and concerns. We want to be sure that all of the students are sharing and collecting the same information.

Please open the data file and edit the telephone script that I left on your desk. Set it up like a report, but adjust margins or whatever to keep it on one page. Apply styles as shown to emphasize the parts of the conversation.

Thanks.

Elect William Wright, Jr. Campaign
985 Cherryhill Crescent
Chesapeake, Virginia 23322
(757) 555-0198
electwrightjr.com

TIP...

To apply styles, select the text and apply the desired style from the Formatting toolbar.

Telephone Script

] TELEPHONE SCRIPT [

Opening (Heading 1)

Good Evening (*name*) _____. I am calling for William Wright, Jr., who is running for Mayor of Chesapeake. May I ask what you think of Mr. Wright?

Response (Heading 2)

FAVORABLE, SAY . . .

That's great. William Wright needs every vote.

\#

UNFAVORABLE, SAY . . .

Thank you for your time and courtesy. Good evening.

\#

UNDECIDED OR DON'T KNOW, SAY . . .

Let me tell you why I'm working so hard for him. William Wright has been an independent and effective voice in our city. He will work for and with our citizens to improve our city.

What's more, Candidate Wright is very interested in the issues and concerns of the youth in our city. He wants to hear from every youth. What are some of the issues or concerns that you feel Candidate Wright should focus on during his campaign and after he is elected?

\#

AFTER THE ISSUES AND CONCERNS HAVE BEEN IDENTIFIED:

Thank you for your candid response. You can be assured that this information will be passed on to Candidate Wright and responded to during the campaign. We need a man like William Wright in Chesapeake to get our city moving in the right direction.

Closing (Heading 1)

Is there anything else you ~~might~~ want to know about William Wright, Jr.?

Thank you for your time. Please be sure to vote on Election Day and remember,

"What a Difference "A" Vote Makes!" **14-pt. bold**

From: Victor McBride [vmcbride@electwrightjr.com]
To: STUDENT [student@electwrightjr.com]
Date: Friday, March 28, 200- 11:56 AM
Subject: Volunteers

I've left a list of volunteer campaign workers on your desk. Please format them in a table. The title of the table should be HIGH SCHOOL VOLUNTEERS. Use the following column headings: Telephone, Canvasser, Fundraising, Office, Mailings, and Miscellaneous. Insert the name, address, and school of each worker in the appropriate column. Abbreviate the school name by using HS instead of spelling it out. Format the table attractively.

Thanks.

Elect William Wright, Jr. Campaign
985 Cherryhill Crescent
Chesapeake, Virginia 23322
(757) 555-0198
electwrightjr.com

TIP...

Use landscape orientation. Change left and right margins to 0.5". Use a 10-pt. font and abbreviate where necessary so lines don't wrap. Shade column heading row. Center column headings.

High School Volunteers

Ms. Gail Johnson
1666 Stoney Avenue
Chesapeake, VA 23321
Chesapeake High School
Telephone

Ms. Tricia Adamson
3829 Woolard Drive
Chesapeake, VA 23321
Oscar Green High School
Canvasser

Mr. Travis Johns
382 Hickory Road
Chesapeake, VA 23325
Chesapeake High School
Fundraising

Mr. Patrick Persons
382 University Drive
Chesapeake, VA 23322
Chesapeake High School
Fundraising

Miss Lydia Clinton
932 Starr Drive
Chesapeake, VA 23325
Oscar Green High School
Office

Mr. Perry Nash
10 College Drive
Chesapeake, VA 23325
Oscar Green High School
Mailings

Mr. Alexander James
3856 Middletown Crescent
Chesapeake, VA 23320
Eastern Branch High School
Telephone

Mr. Leroy Blue
310 Berrypick Lane
Chesapeake, VA 23322
Eastern Branch High School
Mailings

Mr. Walter Baker
1707 Birch Trail
Chesapeake, VA 23323
Grassfield High School
Mailings

Mr. Robert Mann
3554 Lloyd Drive
Chesapeake, VA 23325
Eastern Branch High School
Office

Mr. Rinji Shinoda
1456 Spring Meadows
Chesapeake, VA 23324
Grassfield High School
Telephone

Mrs. Josie Brown
1910 Springfield Avenue
Chesapeake, VA 23325
Oscar Green High School
Miscellaneous

Ms. Shirley White
2805 Lyndora Road
Chesapeake, VA 23323
Indian Cove High School
Canvasser

Mr. George Bruce
5548 Woodside Court
Chesapeake, VA 23321
Grassfield High School
Office

Ms. Harriet Coleman
2923 Brideshead Crescent
Chesapeake, VA 23321
Indian Cove High School
Mailings

Mrs. Ethel Clemson
6801 Cedar Road
Chesapeake, VA 23320
Indian Cove High School
Miscellaneous

Mrs. Robin Melvin
804 Villanova Avenue
Chesapeake, VA 23321
Grassfield High School
Telephone

Ms. Thelma Echols
3821 Tajo Landing
Chesapeake, VA 23320
Eastern Branch High School
Office

Mrs. Millicent Finney
4961 Dock Landing Road
Chesapeake, VA 23321
Grassfield High School
Mailings

Mr. Perez Chavez
4832 Mill Dam Road
Chesapeake, VA 23321
Grassfield High School
Telephone

ELECT WILLIAM WRIGHT, JR. CAMPAIGN

FROM THE DESK OF VICTOR MCBRIDE

March 28

The form containing the information collected from the telephone poll is attached. Please key it in a table and format appropriately. Print one copy. Remove lines. Print another copy. You don't need to save the copy without lines.

Thanks.

Victor

985 Cherryhill Crescent ★ Chesapeake, Virginia 23322 ★ (757) 555-0198 ★ E-mail:

TIP...

Use AutoFit to fit the table to the contents. Be sure to center the table horizontally afterward.

SOFTWARE FUNCTIONS: Create and Modify Tables, AutoFit

TELEPHONE POLL RESULTS
of
High School Students

Crime	Females	Males	Total
School Violence	50	45	
Drugs	35	48	
Abuse	25	37	
Homelessness	21	30	
Environment	47	49	
Healthcare	15	13	
Employment	36	18	

ELECT WILLIAM WRIGHT, JR. CAMPAIGN

FROM THE DESK OF MARKITA LAWTON

March 28

Please format and key an attractive flyer from the draft that I have left for you. Insert a border around the flyer and a shading color to compliment the flyer. Choose shading that is light enough that the text is easy to read. Use various fonts and font effects. Set all margins at 0.5". Save this as a Web page.

Thanks for your help.

Markita

985 Cherryhill Crescent ★ Chesapeake, Virginia 23322 ★ (757) 555-0198 ★ E-mail: electwrightjr.com

Cast Your Vote for William Wright, Jr.

on

Election Day, May 7, 200-

for

MAYOR OF CHESAPEAKE

He listens to the voice of our youth and will address your issues and concerns.

School Violence

Crime

Drugs

Homelessness

The Environment

Healthcare

Employment

WHAT A DIFFERENCE "A" VOTE MAKES!

ELECT WILLIAM WRIGHT, JR. CAMPAIGN

FROM THE DESK OF JAMIE ROMBERG

A copy of April's expense report is in a folder on my desk. Please key the information in a table. Total the report. Format the table appropriately.

Thank you.

Jamie Romberg

985 Cherryhill Crescent ★ Chesapeake, Virginia 23322 ★ (757) 555-0198 ★ E-mail:

TIP...

Create a 5-column, 11-row table. Bold the heading row. Center text in header row. Insert formulas to get the totals.

```
           Elect William Wright, Jr. Campaign
                    Expense Report
                 Month of April 200-
```

Expense Item	Week 1	Week 2	Week 3	Week 4
Advertising	21,765.13			796.03
Supplies	274.81			151.09
Telephone	149.81			
Transportation	594.16	67.87	397.07	279.18
Salaries	2,000.00		2,000.00	
Rent	500.00			
Utilities	175.00			
Entertainment	675.00	183.15	212.15	549.83
Miscellaneous	256.00	17.96	121.11	93.10
Totals				

From: Markita Lawton [mlawton@electwrightjr.com]
To: STUDENT [student@electwrightjr.com]
Date: Wednesday, April 2, 200- 11:56 AM
Subject: Commissions

Please key the attached Descriptions of Boards and Commissions with Youth Members. Insert a fancy bullet or symbol for each of the four items describing the board or committee. Bold the board/committee names.

Thank you.

Elect William Wright, Jr. Campaign
985 Cherryhill Crescent
Chesapeake, Virginia 23322
(757) 555-0198
electwrightjr.com

TIP...

For fancy bullets or symbols, choose Customize in the Bullets and Numbering dialog box. Choose either Font or Symbol and make your selection.

CITY OF CHESAPEAKE

Descriptions of Boards and Commissions with Youth Members

Museum Advisory Board
- Advises City Council in the development and use of the museum
- Consists of nine members
- Serves three-year terms (student will serve one-year term)
- Meets third Wednesday of each month

Animal Shelter Advisory Committee
- Advises the city regarding animal shelter issues
- Consists of four members
- Serves two-year terms (student will serve one-year term)
- Meets second Tuesday of each month

Youth Services Advisory Board
- Provides a resource to youth in communicating with their elective representatives
- Consists of nine members
- Serves three-year terms (student will serve one-year term)
- Meets third Monday of each month

Environmental Affairs Board
- Acts in an advisory capacity on matters relating to air pollution, soil contamination, hazardous waste disposal, and other related environmental issues
- Consists of seven members
- Serves two-year terms (student will serve one-year term)
- Meets fourth Thursday of each month

Parks and Recreation Advisory Board
- Advises City Council and Parks and Recreation Director on matters relating to parks and recreation program
- Consists of nine members
- Serves three-year terms (student will serve one-year term)
- Meets first Friday of each month

From: Jason Tuber [jtuber@electwrightjr.com]
To: STUDENT [student@electwrightjr.com]
Date: Wednesday, April 2, 200- 11:56 AM
Subject: Political Jokes

Use the Internet to see if you can find about five to seven political jokes. Set this up as a double-spaced report; use the title Political Jokes. Number each joke and include the Web address centered in a second color below the joke. Make everything consistent including fonts, indents, spacing, and so on.

Thank you.

Elect William Wright, Jr. Campaign
985 Cherryhill Crescent
Chesapeake, Virginia 23322
(757) 555-0198
electwrightjr.com

Use http://www. askjeeves.com, http://www.google.com, or other search engines. Select the jokes and use Copy and Paste to paste them into a Word document. Use Copy and Paste to include the Web address. Use Select All to change the font to Times New Roman 12.

SOFTWARE FUNCTIONS: **Internet**
Search, Copy and Paste

From: Markita Lawton [mlawton@electwrightjr.com]
To: STUDENT [student@electwrightjr.com]
Date: Thursday, April 3, 200- 11:12 AM
Subject: Voting Puzzle

Just for fun, let's see how voting savvy you are. Try completing the Voting Puzzle I left on your desk.

Enjoy!

Elect William Wright, Jr. Campaign
985 Cherryhill Crescent
Chesapeake, Virginia 23322
(757) 555-0198
electwrightjr.com

ARE YOU VOTING SAVVY?

ACROSS

1 A ballot used for voting at home before the election instead of at your polling place.
2 To be allowed to do or get something.
3 A person who is trying to get elected.
4 The place where you go to vote.
5 The spring election on even numbered years that helps parties choose their candidates.
6 When you sign your name.

DOWN

1 A form you mark when you vote.
2 The work people do to get someone elected or to get a ballot measure passed.
3 When people vote to make choices about their government.
4 To sign up; to get on an official list.

Reference Manual

ELECT
WILLIAM WRIGHT, JR.
MAYOR

OPEN FORUM

Come out to talk with the candidate and discuss your concerns.

Monday, June 20, 200-
7:00 p.m.

Riverside Civic League
389 Northside Drive

Letterhead

ELECT WILLIAM WRIGHT, JR. CAMPAIGN

What A Difference "A" Vote Makes!

985 Cherryhill Crescent ★ Chesapeake, Virginia 23322 ★ (757) 555-0198 ★ E-mail: electwrightjr.com

2" or center page

Current date

October 11, 200- ↓4

Letter address

Mrs. Christine Hwang
121 Central Boulevard
Chesapeake, VA 23325-3106 ↓2

Salutation

Dear Mrs. Hwang ↓2

Body

Thank you for your generous contribution of $200 to my mayoral campaign on November 9, 200-. ↓2

I sincerely appreciate your show of confidence in my ability to work for this city and I look forward to your continued support as we move toward Election Day. If there is any way in which I can be of assistance to you, please feel free to contact me at the address above. "My only interest is YOU!" ↓2

Default side margins

Complimentary closing

Sincerely ↓4

Name and title

William Wright, Jr.
Candidate ↓2

Reference initials

rra ↓2

Enclosure notation

Enclosure

Mrs. Christine Hwang   **Header with name,**
Page 2   **page number, and date**
October 11, 200-

We are looking forward to a long and rewarding relationship with you, your students, and your school. ↓**2**

Sincerely ↓**4**

William Wright, Jr.
Candidate ↓**2**

rra ↓**2**

Enclosure

Addressing Procedures

To automatically add the address of a displayed letter to an envelope, use the Envelopes and Labels feature. An alternative style for envelopes is uppercase with no punctuation.

Elect Wright Campaign
985 Cherryhill Crescent
Chesapeake, VA 23322

Mrs. Christine Hwang
121 Central Boulevard
Chesapeake, VA 23325-3106

Alternative format

ELECT WRIGHT CAMPAIGN
985 CHERRYHILL CRESCENT
CHESAPEAKE VA 23322

MRS. CHRISTINE HWANG
121 CENTRAL BOULEVARD
CHESAPEAKE VA 23325-3106

Memo

ELECT WILLIAM WRIGHT, JR. CAMPAIGN

What A Difference "A" Vote Makes!

MEMORANDUM

2"

Heading

TO: tab 1" Markita Lawton, Campaign Manager ↓2

FROM: Brenda Smithwick ↓2

DATE: August 15, 200- ↓2

SUBJECT: Retreat ↓2

Body

I am planning to attend the retreat on October 18 and 19. However, I will arrive approximately one hour late. I am attending a meeting that will require me to leave for Williamsburg later. ↓2

I trust that this is acceptable with you. I will meet with you or one of the other members of the staff later to get whatever information I miss. ↓2

Default side margins

Reference initials

rra ↓2

Copy notation

c Mark Benneton

tab 0.5"

2"

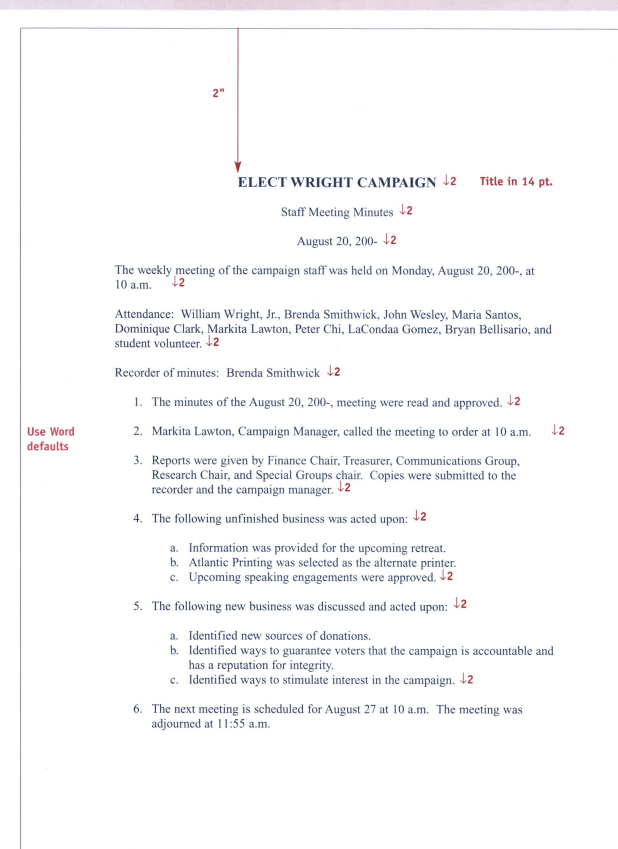

ELECT WRIGHT CAMPAIGN ↓2   Title in 14 pt.

Staff Meeting Minutes ↓2

August 20, 200- ↓2

The weekly meeting of the campaign staff was held on Monday, August 20, 200-, at 10 a.m.   ↓2

Attendance: William Wright, Jr., Brenda Smithwick, John Wesley, Maria Santos, Dominique Clark, Markita Lawton, Peter Chi, LaCondaa Gomez, Bryan Bellisario, and student volunteer. ↓2

Recorder of minutes: Brenda Smithwick ↓2

1. The minutes of the August 20, 200-, meeting were read and approved. ↓2

Use Word defaults

2. Markita Lawton, Campaign Manager, called the meeting to order at 10 a.m.   ↓2

3. Reports were given by Finance Chair, Treasurer, Communications Group, Research Chair, and Special Groups chair. Copies were submitted to the recorder and the campaign manager. ↓2

4. The following unfinished business was acted upon: ↓2

    a. Information was provided for the upcoming retreat.
    b. Atlantic Printing was selected as the alternate printer.
    c. Upcoming speaking engagements were approved. ↓2

5. The following new business was discussed and acted upon: ↓2

    a. Identified new sources of donations.
    b. Identified ways to guarantee voters that the campaign is accountable and has a reputation for integrity.
    c. Identified ways to stimulate interest in the campaign. ↓2

6. The next meeting is scheduled for August 27 at 10 a.m. The meeting was adjourned at 11:55 a.m.

Use the columns feature of Microsoft Word to create newsletters. Use various font styles and sizes, lines, and graphics for special effects. A simple, uncluttered design with a significant amount of white space is recommended to enhance readability.

ELECT WILLIAM WRIGHT, JR.
FOR MAYOR

What A Difference "A" Vote Makes!

Volume 1, Issue 1   Fall 200-

MEET THE CANDIDATE

Once again, the "Wright" man has entered the race; this time for mayor! William Wright, Jr., is following in his father's footsteps in the political arena. But have no doubts, he is definitely his own man.

Wright is a graduate of Chesapeake High School and Hampton Roads University where he received an undergraduate degree in political science and a law degree. He is currently a partner in the firm of Wright and Cherry, attorneys who specialize in entertainment and sports law.

Candidate Wright has been very active in the life of this city and its citizens. He chose to attend college in his hometown and to remain here. While attending Hampton Roads University, Wright was politically active. He also managed the campaigns of two students running for president of the school's student government. In addition, he served the city in various capacities during his father's administration.

Candidate Wright is single. He is a "big brother" to a special little boy who he met through Big Brothers and Big Sisters, Inc.

THE ISSUES

Candidate Wright is concerned about the citizens of this city. His issues include public safety and security, neighborhood improvement, education, government accountability, economic growth, and fiscal stability. He also believes that the concerns and opinions of the youth of our city are especially important; he sees our youth as our future. He promises to involve young people in his campaign and to learn about and address their concerns.

16-pt. Arial, underlined

NEWS RELEASE

12-pt. Arial right aligned

Elect Wright Campaign

10-pt. Arial right aligned

985 Cherryhill Crescent
Chesapeake, Virginia 23322

↓2

Contact: Markita Lawton ↓2

Phone: (757) 555-0198 ↓2

14-pt. bold and centered

FOR IMMEDIATE RELEASE ↓2

Bold

CHESAPEAKE, VA, February 6, 200-—On February 1, William Wright, Jr., held a news conference at 1:00 p.m. on the steps of City Hall to announce his candidacy for the mayor of Chesapeake.

On January 27, 200-, Mr. Wright filed petitions containing more than 70,000 signatures of registered voters in the city of Chesapeake. These petitions qualified Mr. Wright as the first candidate to be placed on the ballot.

A graduate of Chesapeake High School and Hampton Roads University, Wright has always been interested in politics and history. He was active in HRU politics and managed the campaign of two candidates for student government president. He was also involved in city political activities during his father's administration and has represented the city on various occasions. Wright feels that he owes a great deal to the people of this city. If elected, he will do the best possible job to improve his hometown. Wright hopes to build a coalition of support from a broad segment of the community and to fairly represent each segment.

Default side margins

Wright's concerns are the concerns of the people of the city, and he very much wants to hear from residents. ↓2

\####

Set a decimal tab at 0.25" to align the roman numerals. Set left tabs at 0.5" and 0.75" to indent the subheads.

2"

THE CANDIDATE ↓2   Title in 14-pt. bold

I.   BACKGROUND ↓2

    A. Personal
       1. Single
       2. "Big Brother" to Josh O'Quinn
    B. Education
       1. High School Diploma from Chesapeake High School
       2. BA in Political Science and Law Degree from Hampton Roads University ↓2

II. ISSUES AND CONCERNS ↓2

    A. Education
    B. Neighborhood Improvement
    C. Public Safety and Security
    D. Fiscal Stability
    E. Economic Growth
    F. Government Accountability

Proofreading Techniques

It is very important that all documents are error-free. Even though the software will automatically correct some errors and display some misspelled words and grammatical errors, it is necessary for you to proofread your document carefully. In addition to checking the document for errors, also be sure that the document format is correct.

Follow these steps to ensure the accuracy of your documents:

- Correct all errors displayed by the Spelling and Grammar check.
- Scroll through the document to make sure that you have corrected all of the displayed errors.
- Use Print Preview to view the entire document to ensure that all formatting is correct. Check margins, spacing, headings, paragraphs, headers, footers, page numbers, horizontal or vertical centering, and the overall appearance of the document.
- Because proofreading documents on the screen can be difficult, print the document (double-spaced if possible).
- Use a straight edge (i.e., a ruler or an envelope) to help keep your eyes focused on the correct line.
- Read the document word for word. Pay special attention to proper names, correct word use (cite, site, or sight), punctuation, additions, and omissions. Sometimes it is helpful to read the lines backwards, from right to left.
- Mark all errors using appropriate proofreaders' marks.
- Correct all errors and save the document with the corrections.

Proofreaders' Marks

Mark	Symbol		Mark	Symbol	
Align	//		Insert space	/#	
Bold	∼∼∼		Let stand, ignore correction	stet	or ...
Capitalize	cap or ≡		Lowercase	/ or lc	
Center copy	] [		Move down		
Close up	⌣		Move up		
Delete	℘		Move right		
Double space	DS		Move left		
Insert	^		Paragraph	¶	
Insert apostrophe	⌄		Single space	SS	
Insert comma	⌄		Spell out	sp	
Insert period	⊙		Transpose	∼ or tr	
Insert quotation marks	⌄ ⌄		Underline or italics	___	

2"

PROFESSIONAL DEVELOPMENT ↓2 **Title in 14-pt. bold**

When a company purchases new equipment, those who use the equipment will most likely need training. Often the vendors will offer short training sessions to help users become comfortable with their new equipment. However, this training session cannot get deeply involved in the use of specific applications of software packages. So it

Default side margins → is wise for those users to seek additional training. They can obtain information from publications and can participate in hands-on training through special seminars, training sessions, and user groups.

This is only one aspect of professional development. If you want to be the best employee possible, you must continue to stay abreast of the new happenings in office technology. There are several ways to accomplish this.

Professional Journals

There are many trade and professional journals available in the field of office technology, including *Administrative Management* and *The Office*. Because there are so many journals on the market, it is important to review the types of articles in each one to determine which would best meet your needs. The cost of the journal would also be a factor in determining your choice.

Professional Organizations

There are various professional organizations available for office personnel to join. Your membership in professional organizations gives you the opportunity to meet others

↑ **1" bottom margin**

1/2"

1"

2

in your field and share information and experiences. You also have the opportunity to learn what is happening from the specialists in your field. Because there is usually a membership fee, you need to choose carefully which organization(s) you would like to join. If you are to receive the benefits available with your membership, you need to be active and take advantage of the organization's services and opportunities.

Equipment Vendors

Many vendors of office technology equipment sponsor trade shows and fairs. It is to your advantage to attend the shows that would be beneficial to you and your professional development.

Computer Groups

If you use a computer, consider joining a user group. There you will have the opportunity to share information and experiences concerning your computer and software. It helps to know that others have the same problems and concerns that you do, and often you will be able to find a solution together.

If you want to be the best that you can be in your job and make yourself valuable to your employer, you need to be serious about your professional development.

1" bottom margin

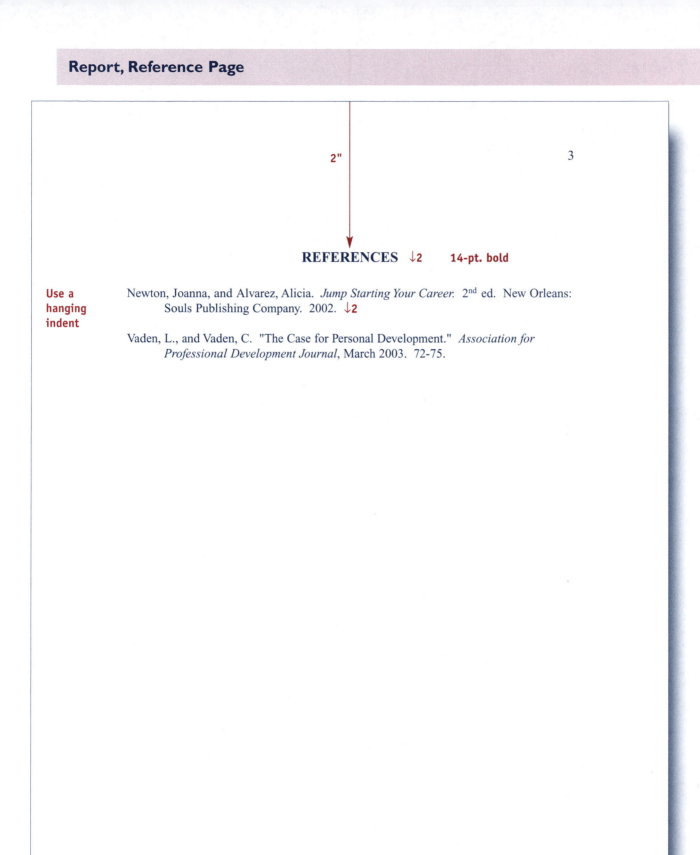

2"   3

REFERENCES ↓2   **14-pt. bold**

Use a hanging indent   Newton, Joanna, and Alvarez, Alicia. *Jump Starting Your Career.* 2nd ed. New Orleans: Souls Publishing Company. 2002. ↓2

Vaden, L., and Vaden, C. "The Case for Personal Development." *Association for Professional Development Journal*, March 2003. 72-75.

↑
1" bottom margin

Center table vertically or DS before and after.

ELECT WRIGHT CAMPAIGN ↓2		
Promotional Items ↓2		
Category	**Number on Hand**	**Number Ordered**
Bumper Stickers	360	500
Posters	75	100
Buttons	437	250
Book Markers	237	175
Key Chains	135	300
Pamphlets	178	225
Total	1,422	1,550

Heading centered in 14-pt. bold

Bold and center →

0.5" →

↑ Right align numbers ↑

Table with lines.

ELECT WRIGHT CAMPAIGN

Promotional Items

Category	**Number on Hand**	**Number Ordered**
Bumper Stickers	360	500
Posters	75	100
Buttons	437	250
Book Markers	237	175
Key Chains	135	300
Pamphlets	178	225
Total	1,422	1,550

0.5" →

Table without lines.

2"

SPEAKING SCHEDULE ↓2   **Title in 14-pt. bold**

Week of August 15, 200- ↓2

August 15, 200- ↓2

Tab at 0.25" ➡ 7:00 p.m.   **Tab at center** ➡ Norfolk High School PTA
                                                      Tanner Creek Lane
                                                      Chesapeake, VA 23513
                                                      555-0114 ↓2

August 16, 200- ↓2

        12:00 p.m.   Mamie Holt Garden Club
                                        928 Johnston Road
                                        Chesapeake, VA 23513
                                        555-0182 ↓2

        7:00 p.m.   Lambert's Cove Civic League
                                        973 W. 37th Street
                                        Chesapeake, VA 23508
                                        555-0189 ↓2

August 17, 200- ↓2

        6:30 p.m.   Bramble Senior Citizen Home
                                        6616 Stoney Point Crescent
                                        Chesapeake, VA 23502
                                        555-0109 ↓2

August 18, 200- ↓2

        7:00 p.m.   Oceanview Civic League
                                        897 Bay Avenue
                                        Chesapeake, VA 23513
                                        555-0142

Data files for completing various jobs are recorded on the CD in the back of this book or your instructor will make them available for your use. Open the data files and then save the file with the name of the job in which it will be used.

 This icon alerts you that a data file is needed to complete a specific job.

Absentee Voting	Job 21
Campaign Issues	Job 8
Certificate	Job 22
Job Descriptions	Job 6
Letterhead.dot	Job 5
Memo.dot	Job 14
News Release	Job 13
Newsletter	Job 19
Precinct Leaders	Job 15
School Board Meeting	Job 12
Summit Budget	Job 17
Summit Program	Job 4
Telephone Script	Job 24

Command Summary

Command	Menu	Toolbar	Shortcut Keys
Align	Format/Paragraph	✔	
AutoCorrect	Tools/AutoCorrect Options		
Bold	Format/Font	✔	Ctrl + B
Borders	Format/Borders and Shading	✔	
Bullets and Numbering	Format/Bullets and Numbering	✔	
Center Page	File/Page Setup/Layout		
Character Effects/Styles	Format/Font		Ctrl + Shift + F
Close	File/Close		
Columns	Format/Columns	✔	
Copy	Edit/Copy	✔	Ctrl + C
Cut	Edit/Cut	✔	Ctrl + X
Date and Time	Insert/Date and Time		
Delete	Backspace or Delete Key		
Exit	File/Exit		Alt + F4
Find/Replace	Edit/Find/Replace		Ctrl + F; Ctrl + H
Font Size	Format/Font	✔	Ctrl + Shift + > or <
Graphics	Insert/Picture		
Indent & Hanging Indent	Format/Paragraph	✔	
Insert	Insert Key		
Italic	Format/Font	✔	Ctrl + I
Line Spacing	Format/Paragraph	✔	
Margins	File/Page Setup		
New	File/New		Ctrl + N
Open	File/Open	✔	Ctrl + O
Page Breaks	Insert/Break		Ctrl + Enter
Page Numbers	Insert/Page Numbers		
Page/Zoom Full	View/Zoom/Full Page	✔	
Paragraph Styles	Format/Styles and Formatting	✔	

Continued on page 82

Command	Menu	Toolbar	Shortcut Keys
Paste & Paste/Special	Edit/Paste or Paste Special	✓	Ctrl + V
Print	File/Print or Toolbar	✓	Ctrl + P
Print Preview	File/Print/Print Preview	✓	
Ruler	View/Ruler		
Save	File/Save	✓	Ctrl + S
Save As	File/Save As		F12
Shading	Format/Borders and Shading		
Show/Hide		✓	
Spell Check	Tools/Spelling and Grammar	✓	F7
Suppress Page Number	Insert/Page Numbers		
Tables	Table/Insert Table	✓	
Tabs	Format/Tabs or Horizontal Ruler		
Template	File/New		
Thesaurus	Tools/Language		Shift + F7
Underline	Format/Font	✓	Ctrl + U
Undo/Redo	Edit/Undo or Redo	✓	Ctrl + Z; Ctrl + Y
Web Pages	File/Save As		
Widow/Orphan	Format/Paragraph/Line and Page Breaks		

Microsoft Word Core Competencies Correlation

	Skill Sets and Skills Being Measured	Jobs
W2002-1	**Inserting and Modifying Text**	
W2002-1-1	Insert, modify, and move text and symbols	1, 13
W2002-1-2	Apply and modify text formats	2, 13, 22
W2002-1-3	Correct spelling and grammar usage	All jobs
W2002-1-4	Apply font and text effects	Most jobs
W2002-1-5	Enter and format Date and Time	5
W2002-1-6	Apply character styles	1, 2, 4, 13, 22, 27
W2002-2	**Creating and Modifying Paragraphs**	
W2002-2-1	Modify paragraph formats	2, 4, 6, 9, 15, 18, 21, 22
W2002-2-2	Set and modify tabs	1, 6, 11, 16
W2002-2-3	Apply bullet, outline, and numbering format to paragraphs	7, 9, 29
W2002-2-4	Apply paragraph styles	9, 15, 21
W2002-3	**Formatting Documents**	
W2002-3-1	Create and modify a header and footer	6, 7, 8, 12, 21
W2002-3-2	Apply and modify column settings	4, 19
W2002-3-3	Modify document layout and Page Setup options	4, 5, 7, 8, 12, 21, 22, 25, 27
W2002-3-4	Create and modify tables	3, 10, 25, 26, 28
W2002-3-5	Preview and Print documents, envelopes, and labels	5, 20, 23, 25
W2002-4	**Managing Documents**	
W2002-4-1	Manage files and folders for documents	General Instructions
W2002-4-2	Create documents using templates	5, 14
W2002-4-3	Save documents using different names and file formats	19, 27

Continued on page 84

	Skill Sets and Skills Being Measured	Jobs
W2002-5	**Working with Graphics**	
W2002-5-1	Insert images and graphics	2, 4, 9, 17, 22, 27
W2002-5-2	Create and modify diagrams and charts	17
W2002-6	**Workgroup Collaboration**	
W2002-6-1	Compare and Merge documents	
W2002-6-2	Insert, view, and edit comments	1, 12
W2002-6-3	Convert documents into Web pages	27

Note: Some of the competencies are covered through Standard Operating Procedures (SOP); see the introduction and welcome to *The Candidate* for a list of these procedures.

Job Log

Job No.	Date Completed	Grade	Comments
1			
2			
3			
4			
5			
6			
7			
8			
9			
10			
11			
12			
13			
14			
15			
16			
17			
18			
19			
20			
21			

Continued on page 86

Job No.	Date Completed	Grade	Comments
22			
23			
24			
25			
26			
27			
28			
29			
30			